Contents

Acknowledgement

This booklet is based on materials developed for the Dunston Enterprise Club. Thanks to all the club participants who helped improve those materials and so made this booklet what it is today.

ISBN 978-1535180511

November 2016

Published by Stratagia Limited on behalf of the Business Advisory Bureau Limited.

Why is this guide important?

The writers of this series of guides for new business owners are all micro (0-9 employees) business owners themselves. Between us we have started up many businesses and worked with thousands of start-ups and new business owners. We all agree that successfully starting and running your own business is about learning by doing.

So this guide is about preparing to start up with a bias for action not planning. In fact, most business plans are works of fiction and bear no reality to the practice. It is usually a lot tougher to win enough customers with the right offer than prospective business owners anticipate. This is the reason that many business plans are overoptimistic by inflating the income and the earnings of the business owner.

Only when you have buying customers on a regular basis and you put together a business plan with the real numbers will you truly be able to make sense of what you need to do and achieve to earn a living in your own business.

That is not to say you shouldn't prepare to run your own business by drafting a plan of where you think you'll be going and how you think you'll get there. This draft plan will save you making costly mistakes and the process of continually rewriting it as you learn from real experiences will save you money, increase your income in the future, as well as increase your chances of long-term success.

Our most famous tweet

I have nearly 16,000 followers on Twitter and this one tweet my followers retweet every day. It contains three essential tips:

• Ask for help from a business owner

• Test trade preferably whilst you're still in a job

• Bootstrap don't borrow

This guide doesn't replace any of these three 'must do's' and here's a quick explanation of what they all mean. If you prefer to watch rather than read, this 10 minute video "The Micro Business Champion On Starting Up" makes all of the same points https://www.youtube.com/watch?v=RYoKeaK_m1k.

1. Ask a business owner for help

There is a world of difference between starting up and running your own new business and being a manager or director of a larger business. However well qualified, or business school educated, the skills and know-how of the business owner are unique. So, try to find a business owner to ask for help. Someone that has started and run their own business successfully for a number of years. Even better, ask one who has run a similar business to the one you are going to set up.

Most UK businesses start from home because it's so important to keep costs at the absolute minimum in the early days of trading, certainly until you've got enough paying customers to consider premises. If you must have premises, for example a café or shop, then choose a business owner to help who has started and run a business in these type of premises.

How do you find a business owner to help you? Ask around friends and family for anyone they know who might be the best option.

Social media such as Twitter, LinkedIn and Facebook groups are all great for spotting business owners in different areas of the country from you that may be quite willing to answer your text or email questions or even have an occasional Skype conversation with you.

Your local enterprise agency (you can find them at http://www.nationalenterprisenetwork.org/business-directory/) will probably be able to help identify the business owners who are willing to give something back to new business owners.

There are some excellent national, low cost, membership, support and learning networks that will help you gain the right kind of know-how from other business owners and our favourite in England is Enterprise Nation. Enterprise Nation has a fabulous TV channel and weekly webinars as well as some live events around the country; go to https://www.enterprisenation.com/.

You'll also find business exhibitions really interesting. Many of the stands are often manned by a business owner who, if not in direct competition with your business, will be willing to answer questions at the stand and in some cases strike up a positive relationship for the future.

It's important when looking to get business owners to help you that you've worked out what kind of things that you could give them in return - even if it's just to buy something from them. It can certainly be worth it to offer to pay for an hour or so of their time. If you do the preparation of your questions then just a couple of hours over a few weeks is all that's necessary and will be absolutely invaluable.

This action guide takes you through all the key decision areas, your product/service offer and what you will need to do to survive and thrive. These are all the things that are worth giving a reality check with another business owner.

Make a list here of the business owners you could turn to for help.

Source	Name	Contact details
Family		
Friends		
Enterprise Agency		
Exhibitions		
Social media		
Other		

If you'd prefer to have this, and other worksheets in this introduction, as a separate sheet to fill in you can download them from http://TonyRobinsonOBE.com/action-guide-to-starting-your-business.

2. Test trade first, preferably whilst you're still in a job (have a main source of income)

Our experience is that it usually takes two or three times longer than new business owners expect to gain the number of customers to hit the income figure they need.

Test trading really helps you get your offer to customers right. You will learn more from buying customers than from anyone else. By asking customers the right questions (this is the subject of another guide we are producing) you will learn how they prefer to buy; how to price your product; which product service features and benefits are the most popular and especially the characteristics and behaviours that describe the people most likely to buy your products and services in the future.

We found that prospective business owners who thoroughly test trade often end up starting a business significantly different but significantly more successful than the one they envisaged at the planning stage.

We repeat that starting and running your business is a 'learning by doing' business, which is why investors and bankers aren't the best people to advise. You'll know what you need to do from test trading. If you have started the business already then do consider getting a supplementary form of income such as a part-time job or find some other way so that you can still do some test trading before investing all of your time and money into your business.

The brilliant thing today is that there are so many on-line sales platforms of products, like eBay and Etsy, and for services, such as freelancer.com and people per hour, that you can often test trade online before you start an off-line (and online) business.

Back in the day we only had exhibitions, market stalls and car boot sales but these are all still appropriate. Off-line test trading has been aided too by pop-up shops and trade fairs.

There is no substitute for test trading first, getting real buying customers and asking those customers questions which will provide the know-how for your future success.

Make some quick notes on where you could test trade or people you could approach to be your first 'test trade' customers.

3. Bootstrap - don't borrow

We blame popular TV shows, like Dragon's Den, and the massive television advertising conducted by financial services organisations and government that have almost created an expectation that you need to obtain some funding to start a business. Indeed you could be forgiven for believing that pitching for funding or a loan is an important first skill for a prospective business owner. This is not the case and it is a dangerous misconception. All the authors of this Guide are business owners themselves and we can honestly say that out of the hundreds of successful business owners we know, including some very famous ones that appear on television, we do not know one that started after having pitched for funding. Loans and investors want their money back and most of us don't want this noose around our neck at the very beginning. You need maximum freedom and flexibility until you have built your customer base big enough to know what you need to do to grow further. It is only what you do and what your customers buy in volume that dictates whether you have a viable business or not.

Of course, loans, crowd-funding and investors have their place in helping new business owners develop the business but we feel that it's likely that these will be more of a hindrance than a help in the first 6 months to 18 months of a new business.

This action guide will ensure you have an idea of what you need to do but you need time to do it. Buy yourself the time to get your business on the right track by bootstrapping. Bootstrapping means using friends, family, other business owners, free and low-cost resources, other forms of income, keeping your costs to the minimum and whatever it takes to keep going without the encumbrance of an organisation to whom loans must be repaid or an investor that wants a slice of your action.

Make a few quick notes of the things you think you need to get your business off the ground. Then for each one ask yourself two questions.

• Do I really need this before I start test trading?

• To whom can I turn to beg, borrow or barter for what I need?

What's needed?	Essential to test trade?	Who to beg, borrow or barter with?

In some cases after just six months you'll feel confident about the number of customers you've got and how you've redrafted your plan from this action guide. You'll be able to forecast future income and profitability if you do take a loan or other form of funding to grow your business. In the UK we have the start-up loans scheme (https://www.startuploans.co.uk/) which is ideal when you're at the point where you're not guessing but know what you can make out of your business with the loan.

Proven in practice

Everything in this guide (and all six guides in the @MicroBizMatters series) is proven in practice by new business owners. This is not just from business owners that the authors have helped to start up, although there are very many of those. This guide includes the tips that many business owners we know and have researched found invaluable to a successful start-up.

Each year on the second Friday of January the authors run global #MicroBizMattersDay. This is a day when millions of micro business owners give just a few minutes of their time to help other micro business owners. On the day there is also eight hours of live streamed learning from successful business owners, many of them famous. As a useful supplement to this guide we can recommend you watch the videos of real business owners giving the same proven tips about starting and running your own business.

http://MicroBizMattersDay.rocks

This guide is not theory, it's about actions you need to take in real life. Take the action and learn from it. This guide will take you step-by-step through what you need to do to prepare for and start your own business. However, as we said many times, it is only by doing and learning that you will really be sure that your new business journey reaches its destination

The authors recommend

If you like this action guide then there are five others in this series that you will find very useful for your new business success. They are:

- **Test trading of new products and services**

- **Influencing customers to buy from you**

- **Building profitable customer relationships**

- **Spotting opportunities and making deals**

- **Making your money work for you**

We also recommend that you follow me on twitter @TonyRobinsonOBE as every day we tweet and retweet useful information and contacts to help new business owners.

Our website http://TonyRobinsonOBE.com/action-guide-to-starting-your-business contains all the worksheets in this action guide. Also on the website are many videos, podcasts, blogs, tips, links to useful resources and all the facts about micro businesses in the UK.

Good luck with starting and running your own business. We believe it is a fabulous way of life and of earning a living. Make sure you build your business around things that you enjoy doing because that will keep you going through the harder times. The hard work is always worth it because of the freedom to do your own thing that it gives you.

We know that working through this short guide will help give you the basics and then it's all about learning by doing. So enjoy, learn fast and stay flexible.

All the best,

Tony Robinson OBE
The Micro Business Champion

Navigating this booklet

Starting a business is a process, not an event. Work through the booklet bit by bit as you go along. You can follow it section by section but you don't have to. In the text you'll find ..

KEY POINTS
These are the essential points from each section.

JIGSAW PIECES
Worksheets for you to complete. Fit them all together to give a clear picture of your business.

HELP
Where to go for information and assistance.

BUDDY
Talk through the issue with a trusted business friend.

1 In the beginning ..

- **Keep the faith!**

- **Learn from your experiences, Study – Plan – Act – Review**

- **Set SMART objectives**

Keep the faith!

Ok, you're full of enthusiasm and can't wait to get started with your business idea. This is the best time to take a few minutes to set down why you're starting your business. What do you want out of life and how's your business going to help deliver it? Jot down your reasons in the table below. Two quick rules before you start:

- *You can't just say "to have more money" or something similar.*

If you're tempted to do that, think one step further – what is it that the money will give you? It could be a more reliable car, a house with more room, a holiday, a nest egg for the kids.

- *Your reasons must be positive ones.*

A lot of us start a business to get out of the rat race, away from managers who don't appreciate us and employers who demand more and give less. Turn those negatives in to positives and set down the benefits that your new business will bring you.

Why I'm starting my business - the benefits to give me the life I want

You can download this worksheet from http://TonyRobinsonOBE.com/action-guide-to-starting-your-business

Now for the fun bit. Close your eyes and picture yourself three years from now. It hasn't been a stroll in the park, but your business is thriving. What does success look, smell and feel like? (If that gives you new ideas on why you're starting your business, just add them in to your table).

Look through magazines, your own picture albums, the Internet and anywhere else you can think of. Find images that capture what you want out of your business. Make copies of them, cut them out and stick them together on a sheet of plain paper. It doesn't have to be a work of art! When you've finished, stick your picture up next to your desk, bench or other work station.

Why are we doing this? It's a racing certainty that your pathway to business success will have lots of twists and turns. There'll be setbacks and times when you feel like you're banging your head against a brick wall. Whenever you're feeling low or wondering why you bother, just look at your sheet of pictures. Remember why you're doing this and recapture the motivation you feel today. We'll have more tips to help with this at the end of the booklet.

SPAR

No, you don't have to take up boxing or open a local grocery store. SPAR means

STUDY
Read the Guide and follow through on the links and suggestions it makes so you get to grips with the issues it's raising.

PLAN
Decide what you want to achieve and how you're going to get there.

ACT
Try it out, give it your best shot and see what happens.

REVIEW
Did it all turn out as you planned? What worked well, what didn't and why? How should you change your plans and what could you do to deliver even better results in the future?

Why does this matter?

Most people running a business today had no previous business experience and no prior training in starting a business (or even vaguely related subjects like management).

So how did they learn to run a business? By doing it! They learned from their own experiences, or from people who had done it before. We all think we have great memories, just like we all believe we're one of the best drivers on the road. In practice that's rarely true, so make sure you write down what's important. That way you can look back and see if things worked out as planned. Spotting what worked well and what didn't, and thinking through why, is the best way to build your business and the know how to make it a success. You'll also be amazed at all the things you have managed to get done – don't forget to give yourself a pat on the back when you do!

At the end of this section we've created a worksheet to help you record what you're aiming for and how you're going to get there. Print off as many copies as you like and keep updating it. Before you start using it make sure you've read through the next piece on setting SMART objectives.

SMART objectives

Make sure your goals are set out in a way that makes it easy to say whether or not you've reached your destination. One way of doing this is to set objectives that are SMART. You'll see other versions of this acronym but they're all pretty similar.

Specific
Don't be wooly. Make it clear what the goal is. So 'selling more' isn't much good – specify the particular product, for example.

Measurable
'More' could be just one additional sale. Is that good enough? Try to put a number on it if you can.

Achievable
Make sure you have the resources to get there. Selling an extra fifty days' consultancy services next month isn't going to be possible if you're a one-man band.

Relevant
Make sure the objective fits in with your long-term aims.

Time-bound
Set a time limit for when you're going to do this by.

Now have a go at completing the worksheet on the next page. You may have more than one goal for your business. For example, if you're a hairdresser you may have targets for the number of haircuts and the amount of hair care product you sell each week. Fill in a copy of the worksheet for each of your business goals or objectives.

Continually review what you've written and keep a note of how things are working out and what you've learned along the way.

Remember - be SMART.
Make sure your objectives or targets are Specific, Measurable, Achievable, Relevant and Time-bound.

1 Plan - Act - Review

	Date today		
Where do I want to get to?	What I'm aiming for (be specific)		
	Measure - how many?		
	Deadline date		
How am I going to get there?	Describe what you're going to do and the resources you'll need.		
What was the outcome?			
Why?	What worked well		What didn't work so well

2 Your product and market

- **What's your product?**

- **What do your customers look like and how many are there?**

- **Who are your competitors?**

This section is all about doing the background work to understand who are your potential customers and competitors.

My product

You probably already have an idea of the product you want to sell. If not, look at the sheet on 'Ideas' at http://TonyRobinsonOBE.com/action-guide-to-starting-your-business. Start by providing a description of your product in the next worksheet. If you have more than one product use a separate copy for each one.

There are two versions of the worksheet, one for sales directly to the general public (consumers) and a slightly different one if you're planning on selling your wares to other businesses. Use the one that's most appropriate for your business idea.

My customers

The next step is to think about who is going to buy your product: its market.

If you're selling your product directly to consumers think about the type of people you are aiming at. What best describes them? For example, in terms of:

•Location - e.g where they live or work

•Age

•Sex

•Ethnicity

•Occupation

Depending upon your product, there could be other important characteristics, such as marital status, whether they have children, whether they own or rent their home, physical disability and their values/commitments (e.g. environmentalists, religion, football fans). Add to or amend the worksheet so it works for your business idea.

If you're selling to other businesses then the way you describe them will be slightly different. It could include, for example,

- Location - e.g. where the business is based

- Industry or trade

- Public, private or third sector

- Characteristics of owners

- Scope of business (e.g. are their customers local, regional, national, international)

Try visualising your typical potential customer(s) by adding a drawing or cutting and pasting a picture alongside your description if that helps.

Now try to estimate how many of these people (or businesses) are in your market place. If you need help, try

Consumers

- your local library

- data from the Office for National Statistics at http://www.neighbourhood.statistics.gov.uk/dissemination/.

Businesses

- you can find very basic small business statistics at https://www.gov.uk/government/collections/business-population-estimates.

- market research reports for different industries that are published commercially. These are usually expensive but may be available through your local library, enterprise agency or other business support organisation.

Keep a record of

• where you got information from. It may change in the future and if you keep a note you can always go back there and check

• any assumptions you made. Chances are you'll never find exactly the information you want, so you'll have to make your best estimate. Again, keep a note of how you worked out your estimate so you can update and improve it in the future.

Who are your competitors?

Who else is trying to sell a similar product to people in your market? Try searching the Internet, Yellow Pages, trade magazines, local papers, local shops or other sources to find competitors. You, your family and friends may also have ideas.

There may also be indirect competition. For example, you may be offering a service to repair IT equipment but an alternative could be to buy a new piece of kit. See if you need to add to your list of competitors.

You'll find in the worksheets on the next pages there is an area for prices. We'll return to this in the next chapter so you don't need to fill it in now.

Continually learn and improve

Talk through your ideas with a business buddy.

Keep coming back to what you've written down as you test out your ideas and win your first customers. Things will never work out exactly as expected, so update your notes to take account of what you've learned along the way.

2a Product and consumer market

Product description		
Customer criteria		**Picture**
location		
age		
sex		
ethnicity		
occupation		
other 1		
other 2		
other 3		
How many?		
Sources and assumption		

Competitors	Name	Website or address	Price, £
1			
2			
3			
4			
5			
6			
7			
8			

2b Product and business market

Product description	

Customer criteria		Picture
location		
industry/trade		
sector (public, private, third)		
characteristics of owners		
scope (local, regional, etc.)		
other 1		
other 2		
other 3		
How many?		
Sources and assumption		

Competitors	Name	Website or address	Price, £
1			
2			
3			
4			
5			
6			
7			
8			

3 Pricing your product

- **Work out the price for your product**

- **Don't charge too little when you start**

You can think of pricing your product like a pair of scissors. On the one hand you want the price to be as high as possible to make the most from each sale. On the other hand you might need the price to be low to make as many sales as possible. It's a balancing act.

There are also two sides to the pricing coin. We'll take each one in turn.

Earning enough

There is a very basic question for your business: can you earn enough from selling your product? To do so you need to cover your

- salary or wages

- costs

and earn

- profits

to give you a cushion and cash to invest in future years. Fill in the worksheet on the following page to work out what you need to earn in a year.

Now work out what you need to charge to raise this amount of money.

For services

The following calculator can be used if you're offering consultancy or similar services where the 'product' is sold on the basis of a daily rate for your time.

Divide the Total by 135. This is based on

3 Annual costs and profits

Item	Annual cost, £
Own salary or wage	
Other salaries, wages and sub-contractors	
Tax and National Insurance	
Rent or other premises payments	
Rates	
Electricity	
Gas	
Water	
Telephone	
Internet	
Postage	
Stationery	
Printing and design	
Advertising and marketing	
Travel, hotels, etc.	
Events, exhibitions, etc.	
Professional services (e.g. accountant, bookkeeper, solicitor)	
Insurance	
Subscriptions	
Equipment purchase, hire and maintenance	
Materials and other supplies	
Bank charges	
Other 1	
Other 2	
Profits	
TOTAL	

- 45 weeks (allowing you 7 weeks for public and annual holidays), and
- 3 days (allowing 2 days a week for training, marketing, managing your money, etc.)

Divide again by 7 if you want an hourly, rather than daily, rate.

For products

If you have only one product then this is straight forward – just divide the Total by the number you expect to sell in a year.

If you have more than one product then make your best estimate of the number you expect to sell of each and the price you might charge. For each one work out the annual income by multiplying the number by the selling price. Add up the incomes from each product and adjust the numbers (number sold and/or price) until the incomes add up to the Total you need.

Let's call the price you've calculated so far the Income Price, because it's the price you need to give you the income you want.

My Income Price is £ …………………………………….

Bettering the competition

Go back to Jigsaw Piece 2 in chapter two. You should have a list of competitors for each of your products. Try to find out what they are charging for the kind of products you want to sell and record them in the worksheet (either 2a or 2b).

Given what you know about the quality of your competitor's products and their reputation, work out what would be a reasonable price for you to charge for your product(s). Let's call this price the Competition Price because it's based on what you can charge and be competitive with people selling similar products.

My Competition Price is £ …………………………………….

Is your Income Price lower than your Competition Price?

Yes
Set your selling price somewhere between the two.

My Selling Price is £ …………………………………….

No

If your Income Price is higher than your Competition Price then you have a problem. It means the going rate in your market (the Competition Price) is lower than you need to get by (the Income Price). Check the numbers you have worked from and see if you can reasonably and realistically adjust them to lower your Income Price. If you can't, that's a strong message that your business is unlikely to work. Perhaps it's time to go back to the drawing board and consider what other products you could offer.

Some common mistakes

Perhaps the most common mistake we make when starting a business is to pitch our prices too low. It's natural to worry about getting the first few customers and to think that offering very low prices is the best guarantee of jumping that hurdle. However it causes both an immediate and a longer term problem.

First, potential customers can see this as an indicator of low quality or value to them. So they may actually be put off buying, thinking the price is too good to be true.

Second, it also sends a longer term signal to the market. Once you're established you may want to raise your prices because you're no longer worrying about getting the first few customers. However your existing customers will not be impressed if they see you're offering the same product but now want to charge them a lot more.

One way around this bind is to have an 'introductory offer' or something similar. It allows customers to try out your product without risking so much cash but on the clear understanding that future purchases will be at the normal, higher price.

Final points

As always, try to test out your pricing in a small scale way at the beginning if you can. Always ask for feedback from your customers or potential customers and make any adjustments you think are necessary.

If you're not sure, talk things through with a business buddy.

4 Getting the message out

- **Sell the benefits of your product, not the features or functions**

- **Understand what benefits your customers are looking for**

- **Write to sell**

- **Test and measure to see what works best**

- **Create a sales system, building relationships to deliver sales.**

In this section we're going to look at how you tell potential customers about your product – marketing. There are three key points.

Sell the benefits, not the features

Why is anyone going to buy your product? People will buy it because they get a benefit from it.

A common mistake is to try to sell your wares based on their features or function. It's very easy, if you're an expert in your field or have spent a long time developing your product, to wax lyrical about the features or functions of what you're offering. Don't! **Look at it from the customer's point of view**. What benefit does it give them?

Of course, you'd hope the features will ensure your product delivers the benefits you want. For example, I want a computer that won't freeze or crash. I'd like it to be able to quickly open web pages and cope with the video and other media that now seem to be everywhere. All the stuff about Megahertz and Gigabytes may help the geeks; what I want to see is 'guaranteed not to crash when you're watching your favourite film on DVD' . The features are just a means to an end – it's the benefits you're really after.

To help you get a handle on the benefits of your product we're going to give you two very simple lines of attack. At a very basic, psychological level we do things for one of two reasons

- avoiding pain

- gaining pleasure

Use the worksheet on the next page to list out what your product offers in terms of bringing pleasure or avoiding pain.

Don't worry if all your answers are in one box – use the other box to come up with some creative ideas. For example, when I was little my dentist gave me 'sweets' after a check-up. (Of course, they were not sweets but brightly coloured goodies that actually helped your teeth). I can't say the visit to the dentist was ever a pleasure but you can see how I might think that dentist was better than the rest!

In a similar vein, I use a great local accountant. He helps me stay the right side of the tax man. That saves me a lot of time, money and sleepless nights! When I sit in his office reception I love looking at his book of jokes about accountants. It almost makes it a pleasure, but it's really about avoiding the pain.

So, have a go now at describing the benefits of what you have to offer. If you get stuck you can list the features or functions of your product in the right-hand column. But if you fill in that area, don't stop there. Use what you've written to help you come up with ideas on the benefits of your product.

4 The benefits of your product

avoiding pain	prompts: features or functions
gaining pleasure	

This is also an area where doing a bit of research can pay huge dividends in two ways.

Talk to your customers (or potential customers)

• What do they really want?

• What's wrong with what they are buying at the moment?

• What do they think about your market, the products and the people who provide them at the moment?

For example, common complaints about consultancy firms can be around

– value for money - senior people pitch to get the job but then junior staff do all the work

– timetables slipping

– not delivering to budget

So, if you were in that market place, you might talk about your experience and guarantees about delivering on time and for a fixed budget.

Check out your competitors

A very easy way to do this is to take a look at their website or marketing material – what benefits (or even features) are they pushing?

How can you match them in some areas and do better than them in others? Use your research, experience and feedback to expand and update your 'benefits' table on the previous page.

It's really powerful when you can bring all this together – your ideas, your customers' views and an assessment of your competition's strengths and weaknesses.

At every point in developing your marketing materials, tenders, presentations, etc., refer back to this table and make sure you are really **pushing those benefit buttons**.

Winning words

Most of us need to produce leaflets, brochures and the like to sell our wares. Here are some tips to help make your written material as effective as possible. The principles are also worth bearing in mind when you're writing copy for your newsletter, e-mail or website. Remember - it's about the **CUSTOMER** and how you can make a positive difference to their life.

Put yourself in your customers' shoes. What will your product help them achieve? If you think different groups of customers will have different things they value then think about

- separating your market into different groups or segments along these lines

- producing different sales material for each segment.

For each of the things they really value that you'll deliver

- explain how you and your product/service will deliver it.

  You're really joining the dots for them. We can do this because ...

- give evidence that shows you can deliver.

  Testimonials from satisfied customers are a great way of doing this.

- provide any other information that will deal with any common objections.

If you find it difficult to sort out your ideas, try putting them in a mindmap or spider diagram. Put down the ideas and see how they link to one another. Group similar points together, put them in priority order and think how you're going to link them to one another.

For more information about mind maps see https://en.wikipedia.org/wiki/Mind_map. These are a great way of organising things if you prefer something that's visual to a written list.

Some tips for writing your material

• Don't try to do it all at once. Do the creative, ideas stuff one day; the detailed copy another.

• Use paragraphs to organise your work into a logical series of topics. Keep the first one short to encourage people to read on.

• Each sentence should communicate one idea. If you use 'and' in your sentence, would it be better to cut it into two separate sentences?

• Use short sentences where possible, or a mix of short and longer sentences.

• Commas are handy for lists but don't use lots in a sentence.

• Use present tense and be certain: avoid if, will, can, could, would, .. as far as possible.

• Be active rather than passive. One way is to cut out words ending in ...ing unless they're essential (e.g. bedding plants).

• Don't use lots of different fonts.

• Avoid underlining; use bold to highlight.

• Only use all capitals (e.g short heading) or italics (e.g. captions) in special circumstances.

• Use simple, familiar language (not jargon). Imagine you are talking one to one to the reader.

• Leave some space. Don't make your material overcrowded.

• Pictures can help as long as they are relevant. Before and after pictures can be particularly powerful.

• Try to position the headline/key point a quarter of the way down the page rather than right at the top.

• Finish with a call to action (what you want the reader to do) and give a reason. E.g call us today and claim your free initial assessment.

Check it out - four simple steps

1 Go through your text with a red highlighter or something similar. Highlight all the text that is talking about you and your product/service rather than the customer and what they need. Get rid of the red!

2 Read it out loud. Does it sound right?

3 Ask a friend, colleague or (best of all) a friendly customer to read it. Does it grab their attention? Does it encourage them to read on? Would they respond to the call for action?

4 Edit your copy three times to get it right.

Test and measure

Whatever you do, monitor what the response is. One of the beauties of modern technology is that you can produce small volumes of printed material or change a website at very little extra cost. Try different approaches and see which works best for each of your groups of customers (but try to maintain a consistent approach to help people recognise it's you - in business speak, help build your brand recognition).

Think about the process

You're confident you have a great product. You're certain there are lots of people out there who will love what you have to offer. The only problem is that hardly any of them have heard of you. So – how do you go from having lots of potential customers who don't know you exist through to making the sales that will ensure your business thrives? How can you take people on that sales journey?

People rarely run to purchase something the first time they hear about it. So just putting out one leaflet, posting one advert or hoping your website can sit there and attract customers like bees to a flower isn't likely to work. We need to think of contacting people several times (and, particularly if you're running an on-line business, it's likely to be a lot, lot more!)

People are more likely to buy from those they know and trust. So we need to think about how we can build that kind of relationship.

Think of this as a sales funnel, taking everyone who may be in the market for what you have to offer at the top through to (probably a lot fewer) people at the bottom who have actually become your customer or client. We've summarised the steps along the way as ACTS.

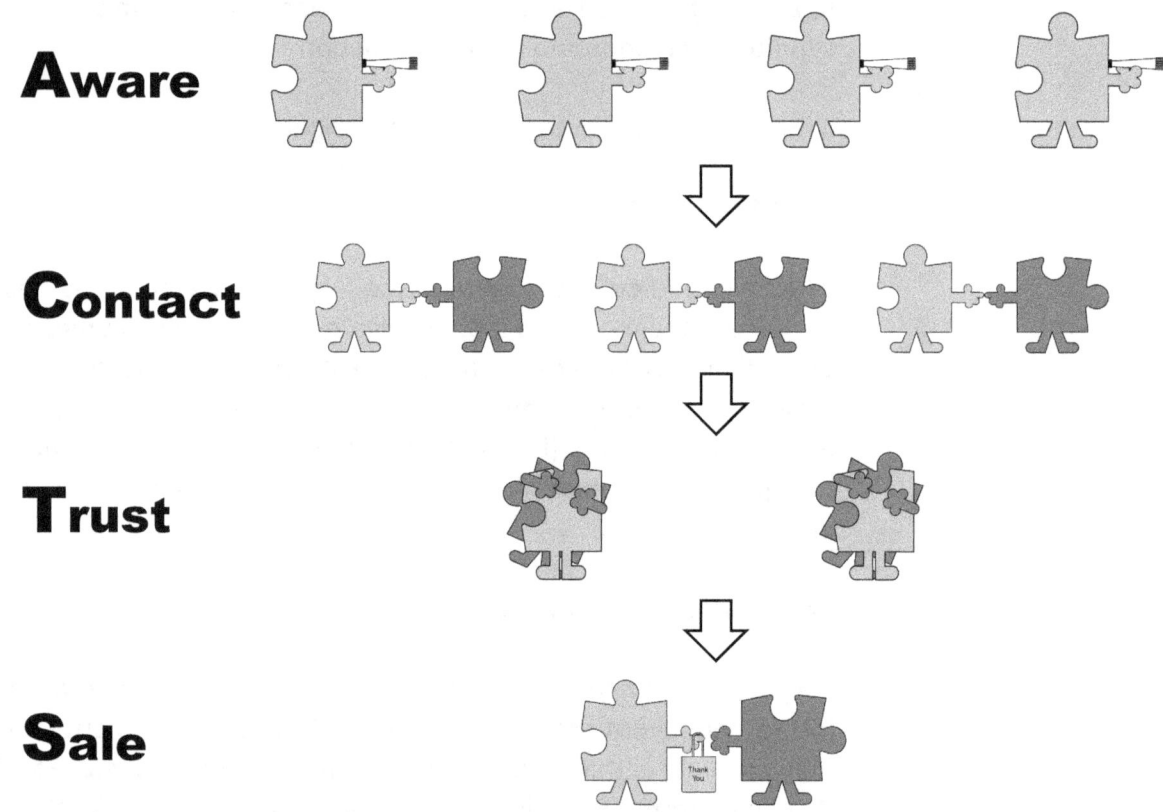

Aware

Contact

Trust

Sale

Let's expand on that a bit.

Aware

Your leaflet, brochure, advert, e-mailing, exhibition, ...helps make some people aware of what you have to offer. Combining and repeating the messages boosts the numbers and heightens that awareness.

Contact

Because you're a good marketer, all your material has a 'call to action' for the reader. That will almost always include a request for people to give you their contact details in return for ...? Well, it could be a free pen, a free information guide, discount on their first purchase, entry into a prize draw or almost anything else that is valuable to them but cheap and easy for you to offer.

Trust

Once you have those contact details you can continue to build an ever-improving relationship by regularly staying in touch with these contacts (and, of course, any existing customers!) That might be a newsletter, for example. Whatever the form, stick to the same principles – try to offer something of value to them that's easy for you to provide. Every once in a while you can include a direct sales pitch but don't do it all the time – think how you would deal with leaflets and e-mails from businesses that were just trying to sell to you all the time. This is your chance to cultivate your image as someone who's expert, friendly and trusted.

Sale

That trust is the best way to achieve a sale. For many small businesses a crucial step is getting to meet the potential customer face to face. Just like you did when winning their contact details in the first place, find a way of making a compelling offer that will encourage your contact to meet up with you.

So, back to our sales funnel. Try filling in the next worksheet to decide how you're going to take your potential customers on that journey from blissful ignorance of what you have to offer through to parting with their hard-earned cash to buy your product. Each part of the worksheet is numbered to link to each of these instructions.

1. Be clear which of your products you are dealing with.

2. Describe the market – what defines or describes the people you are aiming to sell to. Look back at Jigsaw Piece 2 for help.

3. List the possible marketing methods and media you could use: printed leaflets or brochures, adverts, e-mails, telephone calls, exhibitions, ... Try to add detail (e.g. the specific magazine or newspaper you think will be best for your ad). Think of every possible

option and write them down, even if they sound crazy.

4. Decide which methods and media you are going to use. Put a tick against the ones you've selected.

5. Make a note for yourself about why you think each one is or isn't the way to go for what you have to offer. After you've tried a few things you may change your mind, so it's useful to remember what your thinking was originally.

6. Now put your method and media in the order you plan to use them in section 6. In the second column add in what you will be asking them to do. Call you? Meet up? Then in the third column write down what incentive you could offer them.

Make a note of anything else that comes to mind in the final box at the bottom.

Two final tips

• Adapt the worksheet to suit you and your business.

• Don't try to complete the worksheet in one go - this is hard work!

• Test and measure. For each marketing activity keep track of the responses you receive and decide what is and what isn't working for you.

The aim here is to give you a clear programme of marketing activities, an antidote to relying upon one-off activities that always seem to achieve less than you'd hoped for.

More help

If you want more and like working from a book, try *Marketing for Entrepreneurs* by Jurgen Wolff. It's linked to a website with lots of resources.

There is a huge amount of other information on the Internet. A good source is the Marketing Donut, http://www.marketingdonut.co.uk/. Check out videos on You Tube; Stefan Boyle of Print Republic is a good starting point.

5 Marketing plan

1. Product or service	
2. Market Who am I aiming to sell to?	

3. Possible marketing media	4. Use?	5. Why/why not?

6. Links in the chain List the media in the order you plan to use them to move potential customers from people who are unaware of your product/service through to a sale.

media	*action*	*incentive*

Other notes

5 Managing the money

- **Check that your expected income covers what you plan to spend.**

- **Did it? Learn from what actually happened.**

We're now going to go back to look at the money side of the business again. You've already set the price of your product(s) so that your sales should more than cover your costs. There are now two remaining questions:

- is the money coming in at the right time to cover what you're spending?

- have your sales and spending worked out as you expected?

To check this out we're going to create a cash flow forecast. As its name suggests, this is all about

- cash - the money you have in the bank, as well as any notes and coins you may be holding.

- flow - the money coming in and going out of the business.

- forecast - looking ahead to see how you expect the flow of cash to work out in the coming months.

One of the problems when you're starting a business is that you may have expenses to meet before you're able to sell enough of your wares (or be paid for them). **This is one of the main killers of small businesses, so this is important!** Even if you don't like working with numbers, make an exception for this; it will be easier than you think. Your cash flow forecast is your financial early warning system. If there's going to be a shortfall of money in the business your cash flow forecast should tell you, giving you time to do something about it.

You already have all the information you need in section 3, you just need to reorganise it. There's a cash flow worksheet on p.40. There are three points to note.

1. We've set this up with a column for each month. You can alter this to better suit your business.

2. Because of limited space we're only showing two months in the template. You really need this to go on for a year. A full, free version is available as a spreadsheet covering a whole year on our website at http://TonyRobinsonOBE.com/action-guide-to-starting-your-business. This is far and away the best version to use if you can because it's set up to do all the calculations for you - you just need to enter the numbers in the right places. (By the way, if you can't afford the Microsoft Office package that includes Excel there's an excellent and free alternative called Calc available at www.libreoffice.org.)

3. In the worksheet we've labelled the months (the columns) with numbers. Change these in your final version of the cash flow forecast to the names of the months through your financial year. In the income section of the table we've provided five rows for five different products or services (Product 1 to Product 5). Change the names so they are relevant to your business and add in extra rows if need be. These don't even have to be products; they could, for example, be different customers. Just organise and label it the way that's best for your business.

Entering your figures, working out your cash flow

For each month you will see three columns. To begin with just fill in the column labelled 'budget'. This is what you expect to happen in each of the coming months.

To start with fill in the income you expect to earn each month for each product or customer. Make sure you enter the income in the month you expect to receive it. If you have to invoice people for work it could be two months, say, before the money actually appears in your bank account. So, record the month the money is there, not the month you send out the invoice.

Now add in the money you expect to spend each month in the Expenditure section. You've already worked this out for the year in Jigsaw Piece 3 so this shouldn't be too difficult. Again, try to make sure you record these outgoings in the months you actually hand over the cash or when the money leaves your bank account.

Now for a few simple sums. If you're using the spreadsheet from our website you will not need to do this because the spreadsheet should do it for you.

1. Add up all the income you have each month and put the answer in the row labelled A: Total income.

2. Add up all your spending for each month and put that figure in the fourth row from the bottom labelled B: Total spending.

3. In the next row down record the difference between your income (A) and your spending (B). This is your cash flow for the month.

4. At the start of the first month you may already have had some cash in the business, including money in the bank. If so, enter this amount in the next to last row for your first month. This is called the Opening balance - it's just the amount of money you're starting out with at the beginning of the year and each month after that.

5. Now work out how much cash you expect to have at the end of the month - your Closing balance. This is just what you start the month with (D, your Opening balance) plus the cash flow for the month (C). Add C and D together and put the answer for the month in row E.

You can now repeat the final two steps for every month. The Closing balance (in darker grey) one month becomes the Opening balance (in lighter grey) the next month.

Updating your cash flow forecast

So far you've just entered figures in the budget columns, setting down what you expect to happen in the coming months. (We've assumed you're working with months. Just treat this as referring to your chosen time periods if you've opted for something different to better suit your business).

As each month goes by record what actually happened in the second column for each month. If you have a business bank account you can use your statements to check this. If you haven't opened a business bank account yet check out the suggestions at the end of section 7.

Change the rest of your forecast to take account of what actually happended. For the following month use the Closing balance in the Actual column (rather than from the Budget column which you currently have) to be the Opening balance for the following month.

You can now see whether your expectations worked out. Work out the difference between what you expected (Budget) and what actually happened (Actual) for all the entries and put the answer in the Variance column. The spreadsheet version will do this automatically for you.

Learning from the cash flow forecast

Check through to see if there are any big Variance figures. If there are, why did they happen? Do you need to make any changes to the rest of your cash flow forecast?

Look across the closing balances in the Budget column for each future month. Are any of them negative? If so, you really have three options:

- increase your income, either by selling more or raising your prices

- cut (or delay) your spending

- borrow

The last option often seems easiest but can be the most dangerous. Be certain that anything you borrow can be paid back when it's due.

This would be a good point to get ideas from other people you know and trust.

6 Cash flow forecast

Month	1			2		
	budget	actual	variance	budget	actual	variance
Income						
Product 1						
Product 2						
Product 3						
Product 4						
Product 5						
Loans/grants						
Bank interest						
Other						
A: Total Income						
Expenditure						
Own salary or wage						
Other wages & sub-contractors						
Tax & National Insurance						
Rent & other premises payments						
Rates						
Electricity						
Gas						
Water						
Telephone						
Internet						
Postage						
Stationery						
Printing & design						
Advertising & marketing						
Travel, hotels, etc.						
Events, exhibitions, etc.						
Professional services						
Insurance						
Subscriptions						
Equipment purchase, hire, etc.						
Materials & other supplies						
Other spending						
B: Total Spending						
C: Cash flow (A-B)						
D: Opening balance						
E: Closing balance (C+D)						

6 Being organised

- **Value your time**

- **Set priorities for what you need to do**

- **Check where your time goes**

- **Organise your paper and electronic files**

Your time is one of your most valuable assets – make sure you don't waste it! Here are some tips to help.

Create a 'to do' list

Fill in the worksheet in Jigsaw Piece 7, listing all the things you need to do.

- Use the simple scale on the page to say how important each one is.

- Set a deadline by which each one needs to be done.

- Order your list by importance first and then by deadline date, with the earliest dates first.

The point here is to make sure you focus on what's important rather than what's urgent. Does the item with the most urgent deadline really need doing?

A few other tips

1. Put a line through items as you complete them so you can see the progress you're making.

2. Spend five minutes at the end of each day updating your 'to do' list so you're ready to go first thing the next morning.

3. If there's an item you can complete quickly consider doing that first so you get a 'quick win' to increase your motivation and confidence.

4. Do the things you don't like doing early in the day if possible so they are out of the way (rather than hanging over you and the rest of your work).

5. When you have an important piece of work that is going to take hours to complete, block out time in your diary, just like you would if you were making an appointment for a job or meeting. To avoid distractions, turn off e-mail or similar alerts on your computer and 'phone, put a 'do not disturb' notice on your door and divert your 'phones to answerphone (or someone else if that's an option).

6. If you are working in your own office, make sure it's a pleasant and comfortable place to work. Think about using plants, posters and pictures to help achieve that.

Check where your time goes

Do you know how you're spending your waking hours? If you're not sure and you're struggling to complete everything you need to do try keeping a time diary for a week. See Jigsaw Piece 8 for a worksheet.

Record what you do during the day in quarter hour slots. As you record them or at the end of the day, decide whether a time slot was used for paid work (e.g. if you're selling your time as a consultant), other productive work (e.g. meeting a customer, marketing, doing the accounts, making your product) or was non-productive.

We all need a break during the day, so expect some non-productive time when you stop for lunch or a cup of tea/coffee. The question is whether we're spending too much unproductive time, possibly to avoid completing tasks we don't enjoy. Did we put the TV on at lunch time and finish up watching too much day time TV? Did we spend an hour on Facebook when we could have spent five minutes doing what was important for our business? Look at the reasons for your non-productive hours and see what ideas you can come up with for reducing them. For example, are there better times of day to be doing the trickier and more difficult tasks?

Finally, make sure you have plenty of sleep; avoid excessive food, drink and TV; exercise regularly; organise quality time to spend with your family and friends; take breaks and reward yourself for your achievements.

7 To do list

Item	Importance	Deadline	Order
			1
			2
			3
			4
			5
			6
			7
			8
			9
			10
			11
			12

Give Importance a simple score as follows:

1 = critically important, absolutely has to be done

2 = very important, really must be done

3 = important

4 = quite important

We're assuming if any item is less important than this you won't even bother to put it on the list!

You can download this worksheet from http://TonyRobinsonOBE.com/action-guide-to-starting-your-business

8 Time recorder

Time	Activity	Time	Activity
7.30		1.30	
7.45		1.45	
8.00		2.00	
8.15		2.15	
8.30		2.30	
8.45		2.45	
9.00		3.00	
9.15		3.15	
9.30		3.30	
9.45		3.45	
10.00		4.00	
10.15		4.15	
10.30		4.30	
10.45		4.45	
11.00		5.00	
11.15		5.15	
11.30		5.30	
11.45		5.45	
12.00		6.00	
12.15		6.15	
12.30		6.30	
12.45		6.45	
1.00		7.00	
1.15		7.15	

Total paid hours	
Total other productive hours	
Total non-productive hours	

Reasons for non-productive hours	Ideas for reducing non-productive hours

7 Legal and similar stuff

- **Choose the structure for your business**

- **Understand what you need to do to keep the tax man happy**

- **Decide on a bank**

What legal form for your business?

Sole trader
This is where you work as a self-employed person. You can still trade under a business name.

Company
You can set your business up as a company and then become employed by the company.

There are pros and cons to the two options and your judgement on these may differ depending upon who your customers are (consumers or other businesses), how you see the business developing in the future, practice in your industry and attitude to ownership of the business.

Put simply, the **advantages** of setting up as a company are:

- Limited personal liability for any debts

- May look more substantial to potential customers, especially the public sector or other businesses

- Easier to sell or to raise money through selling shares or by other investment

The **disadvantages** are:

- You need to register the company and create formal documents for it

- Bookkeeping/accounts are usually more complicated

That means more costs.

Other options include a partnership, which can also take the form of a limited liability partnership. This is often used in professional practices. You may also want to set up a social enterprise. Typical forms here are companies limited by guarantee (very similar to a limited liability company) or a Community Interest Company.

Some further, but limited, information is available at https://www.gov.uk/set-up-business-uk. You'll find lots more information on this subject on the Internet.

If you're unsure about the best option, talk it through with someone who's started a business before or with an advisor or accountant if you have, or know, one.

Tax - personal

If you opt for self-employment you will need to notify HMRC; see https://www.gov.uk/set-up-sole-trader for more information.

They will also ask you to handle your personal taxation through an annual self-assessment return. The same will happen if you become a director of your own company.

There is a lot of training and advice available from the tax man to help you gear up for dealing with these issues. See http://www.gov.uk/government/collections/hmrc-webinars-email-alerts-and-videos.

Tax – business

If you've set up a company then you will need to register it with HMRC for Corporation Tax (although you have three months to do this).

Another major tax issue is Value Added Tax (VAT). Most, but not all, sales of products or services are liable for VAT. If your sales during a year go over the threshold (£83,000 in 2016-17; check for the latest figure at www.gov.uk/vat-registration-thresholds) then you have to register for VAT.

If your sales don't go above the threshold then you can choose not to register for VAT. There are two possible advantages to this.

1. If you are selling your wares to private consumers (e.g. as a domestic plumber) then your final price is likely to be cheaper than a VAT registered business. With business customers this advantage disappears because most businesses are themselves VAT registered and can recover the VAT.

2. This also means you save time. You don't have to work out what the balance is between VAT you've received and paid out every three months, which then has to be paid to HMRC.

Alternatively you can register for VAT even if your sales are below the threshold. Again there are a couple of possible advantages. First, you'll be able to recover any VAT you've paid out. Second, it can make the business look more established to potential customers. This may be valuable if you are selling to the public sector or big businesses.

Managing money

There are a lot of software packages to help you manage your money. We'd encourage everyone starting a simple business to use one of these and keep their own records. That way you begin to understand the basic principles. Later on you may decide to get help. This could be because you want to free up your time to spend on other jobs. Or perhaps your business has grown and the accounts are getting more complicated.

One option is to use a bookkeeper. Try searching on http://www.iab.org.uk/find-bookkeeper or ask other business owners who they would recommend.

Beyond that you may need to think of using an accountant: see members.accaglobal.com/en/find-an-accountant.html or http://www.icaew.com/en/about-icaew/find-a-chartered-accountant. There are also on-line alternatives available nowadays, such as http://www.cheapaccounting.co.uk/.

This is one area where it will really pay to ask around and seek recommendations from other business owners.

Choosing a bank

First of all, be clear what you want from your bank and the accounts they offer. For example, will you be paying in lots of cash every day or will everyone be paying you through electronic bank transfers? Will you be operating electronic point of sales equipment, taking credit card payments or using facilities like PayPal so people can pay you on-line? Will you be making sales overseas and in different currencies? Do you need a savings account that offers a higher rate of interest?

Once you are clear what kind of service you'll need from a bank

• check out what accounts the different banks are offering – their services, fees and interest rates

• ask other businesses (especially ones that operate like yours) who they bank with and whether they'd recommend them.

Decide which bank and account will best meet your needs.

End note

It's a good idea to keep a note of what you've decided on all these issues and why. That way you can always look back if you think there are reasons for changing how your business operates.

Final notes and information

Support from organisations

There are a wide range of business organisations out there that may be able to help you with information, support and opportunities to make contact with other business owners. We've only listed a few here - do check the Internet, enquire at your local library and ask your contacts for other suggestions.

Enterprise Nation www.enterprisenation.com
There are some free resources here and lots more if you decide the modest membership fee is worth it.

Enterprise Agencies www.nationalenterprisenetwork.org
There are lots of local enterprise agencies and they can be quite different. Check out the national network website, find your local agency and see what they have to offer.

Federation of Small Businesses www.fsb.org.uk
The largest business membership organisation in the UK. Check their website to find out contact and other details for your local branch. Some of their meetings are open to non-members. They frequently have interesting speakers and can be a good way of meeting up with other local business people. They offer a range of services, such as a legal help line, for members.

Chambers of Commerce www.britishchambers.org.uk/find-your-chamber/
The link takes you to the website for the British Chambers of Commerce site, an organisation that represents the individual, local Chambers across the country. Use the link to find your local Chamber. They are also membership organisations offering services to their members but, unlike the FSB, will include businesses of all sizes.

Forum of Private Business www.fpb.org
A membership organisation offering business support resources, legal protection and updates and a collective voice for small businesses.

The Association of Independent Professionals and the Self Employed
www.ipse.co.uk/
Once again, the clue is in the title! A membership organisation offering a legal and tax helpline and a range of information and guidance if you are self-employed.

Internet

There are lots of resources available to help you on the Internet. We've mentioned several of the most useful sites in the earlier text. Another is the StartUp Donut, www.startupdonut.co.uk. Websites are not the only alternative. UK StartUp, for example, have a great Facebook page and Twitter feed.

If you prefer something to watch then search You Tube. There are lots of videos out there covering many of the enterprise essentials you'll need to help your business survive and thrive.

As with any other material on the Internet, do be careful. You can waste a lot of time searching through sources and the information and guidance they offer may not be accurate or appropriate. As always, see if people you know and trust can recommend sources they found useful.

Books

There are lots of business start-up books out there, along with more specialised ones on marketing, negotiating, networking, bookkeeping and almost any business topic you can think of.

Before you spend your hard-earned money on more books

- check out what's available in your local library

- use a good bookshop to check the content before you buy

- take recommendations from your business buddies.

Managing me!

Starting and running your own business is emotional. You invest a lot of yourself in the business and for many of your customers you are that business. Part of what's needed to survive and thrive is your passion for what you're doing. However there will be difficult times when your emotions are in danger of getting the better of you. Here are a few personal tips for finding your way through.

• Look at the picture you created in section 1. Remind yourself why you're doing this and what your business is going to bring you.

• Often you cannot control what happens to you but you can control how you react. If you do suffer a setback, don't let negative emotions overwhelm you. They're your emotions - at least you can be in control of them!

But, I hear you ask, how do you control your emotions?

• Give yourself licence to feel bad! If something has gone wrong or not worked out as you'd hoped you're bound to feel down. Don't pretend everything is ok. Accept what has happened, try to figure out why (so it doesn't happen again) and allow yourself a little time to be angry, frustrated and/or upset. Try the following tips to make sure that doesn't drag on though!

Here are a couple of quotes from Thomas Edison, the inventor of the electric light bulb.

"I have not failed. I've just found 10,000 ways that won't work."
"Our greatest weakness lies in giving up. The most certain way to succeed is always to try just one more time."

• Just because something you tried didn't work doesn't mean you are a failure. It means you're wiser and one step closer to figuring out what will work.

• Always ask yourself positive questions. "What do I need to do to make this work?" rather than "Why can't I get this to work?". Your brain is fantastic. It will come up with all kinds of ideas. Ask negative questions and it will come up with loads of reasons why you're rubbish. Ask positive questions it will offer up all kinds of possible solutions and answers to problems.

• Matter over mind. You've often heard this phrase the other way around but it can also work in reverse. Feeling down, you tend to slump, your shoulders drop and so forth. So do the opposite. Walk tall and sit up straight. Even better, take a brisk walk. You'll feel brighter and ready to tackle the next task.

• Celebrate your achievements!

Finally, try this exercise as soon as you wake up every morning. As you lay in bed, lock your hands together. Now make like a chicken, flapping your arms up and down. If your elbows don't hit the sides of your coffin, it's going to be a good day!

This sounds a lot funnier when delivered by the irrepressible Richard Wilkins. See www.theministryofinspiration.com.

Tony Robinson OBE
is an author, professional speaker and champion of micro businesses. Tony co-founded the global, free-to-join Enterprise Rockers movement and MicroBizMattersDay. You can find out more about Tony at www.tonyrobinsonobe.com, watch his videos at https://www.youtube.com/user/Soculitherz or follow him on Twitter @TonyRobinsonOBE.

Nigel Hudson
has researched how small business owners learn to survive and thrive for over fifteen years. After founding his first business in 2002, he's applied what he's learned to help countless others through Dunston Enterprise Club, the Prince's Trust and as an enterprise coach. You can follow him at @NigelEntRes.

Peter Drury
is an artist/illustrator who trades as PRDArtwork. Peter has had no formal art training whatsoever and just took up artwork as a stress buster 8 years ago. He also helped develop the material in this book as an active member of the Dunston Enterprise Club. Peter had his first solo exhibition in London called "Icons and Legends" in 2012 but also exhibits in his home patch of Sheffield and North Derbyshire. You can follow him on Twitter, @PRDartwork.

Feedback

We'd really welcome your feedback to improve this booklet or say what other publications you'd like to see. Send your ideas to nigel@stratagia.co.uk.

Thanks and good luck!